THE AWFUL TRUTH

GW01458417

Scoular Anderson

Hodder
Children's
Books

a division of Hodder Headline plc

For the staff and pupils of
Innellan Primary School
who

ZLUNK

helped with this book.

Text and illustrations copyright 1999 © Scoular Anderson
Published by Hodder Children's Books 1999

Book design by Joy Mutter
Cover illustration by Scoular Anderson

The right of Scoular Anderson to be identified as the author and
illustrator of the work has been asserted by him in accordance with the
Copyright, Designs and Patents Act 1988.

10 9 8 7 6 5 4 3 2 1

A catalogue record for this book is available from the British Library.

ISBN: 0 340 73617 8

Printed and bound by the Guernsey Press Co. Ltd,
Guernsey, Channel Islands.

Hodder Children's Books
a division of Hodder Headline plc
338 Euston Road
London NW1 3BH

CONTENTS

FUN

JUST WHAT IS IT?

Which of the following people are having FUN?

A This person is enjoying a ride on the ghost-train at the fun-fair so she's having lots of FUN.

Oooooo!

AEEEEEE!

B This person is standing next to a very big dog with bad breath and lots of teeth. He looks as if he's having FUN but he's not.

Nice doggie!

C This person volunteered to have wet sponges thrown at him at the school fete. He's not sure if he's having FUN or not.

HIT TARZAN ON THE NOSE ~ 6 SPONGES FOR 50p

SPLUDGE

SQUELCH

D This person has joined the school rugby club so she's having tremendous FUN.

So you can see that FUN is a funny sort of thing. Some people might think that getting caught in a thunderstorm is GREAT FUN but other people might not.

Some people might think this is FUN.

When you have FUN you also usually have . . .

Blisters, bruises, bumps, broken bones, blood, bashes, scores, gashes, scratches, punctures, thick ears, black eyes, exhaustion, totterings, limps, bites, snivels, flushes, sweats, flurries, fidgets, nerves, jumps, flaps, frothings, hysterics, butterflies, the willies, heebie-jeebies, qualms, blushes, knocking knees, faints, fizzes, itchings, twitchings, tinglings, tremblings, quiverings, squirmings, thrillings, waverings, gulpings in the throat, dampness in the pants, hearts in the mouth, stomach in knots . . .

. . . and you might only be adding an eyeball to your model dinosaur.

Sometimes FUN can stop being FUN and become FUNGE instead.

But so we can take a closer look at people having FUN, we need spies . . .

Here are our spies – HOOT and HOWL, the robotic owls.

Hoot and Howl will hoot with FUN or howl

with FUNGE. They can swivel their heads in any direction . . .

Hoot and Howl are bristling with aerials
and sensors . . .

. . . so they can detect any snigger, titter, giggle
or snort.

They can skilfully fly in any direction . . .

. . . to find out the AWFUL TRUTH about FUN!
Hoot, hoot! Howl, howl!

THE AWFUL TRUTH ABOUT FUN WITH ANIMALS

Hoot and Howl have been making a list of animals that can be FUN.

TREMENDOUS FUN	GIRAFFES, RHINOS, GIANT PYTHONS, CROCODILES, WORMS, SLUGS.
GOOD FUN	PARROTS, CAMELS, DOGS, HORSES.
SORT OF FUN	CATS, GERBILS, STICK INSECTS, RABBITS.
NO FUN AT ALL	SHEEP, WASPS, SHEER

HOOT!

HOWL!

Some animals are tremendous FUN but they are not very convenient to keep.

They would need a big bed to sleep in.

They would make a mess of your garden or park.

Fetch, boy!

They would be difficult to keep clean.

Some very small animals can be tremendous FUN, too, especially sticky, slimy ones that can be dropped into interesting places.

Most animals treat you as a servant and expect you to clean, sweep, wipe, make food, put them to bed etc.

The budgie is FUN when you can watch it play with its toys.

However, the budgie has no manners. It will throw its food on the floor and then use the floor as a toilet.

It's *you* that has to clean up this disgusting mess. This is when FUN becomes FUNGE.

Yuk!

You don't have to clean up after a tortoise but they're not a bundle of laughs either.

Have you heard the one about..?

HOOT AND HOWL'S AWFUL TRUTH REPORT

HOOT! ON... SMALL ANIMALS HOWL!

TINGLE FACTOR	THRILLING FACTOR	OUCH! FACTOR	AAAARGH! FACTOR
★	★		★

Cats can be quite good FUN when they feel like it. They chase things like bits of paper, or string, or wool.

Oh no, the cat's been playing with my jumper!

The trouble with cats is you just don't know what they are thinking about . . .

CAT THINKING ABOUT NOTHING MUCH IN PARTICULAR.

CAT WATCHING AN ABSOLUTELY BRILLIANT GOAL BEING SCORED ON TV.

CAT DREAMING OF WHAT IT IS GOING TO GET FOR TEA.

CAT THINKING ABOUT THE FUN IT'S GOING TO HAVE BASHING THE CAT NEXT DOOR.

CAT THAT'S JUST DISCOVERED IT'S WON THE LOTTERY.

CAT BEING TOLD IT'S POCKET MONEY HAS BEEN STOPPED.

The AWFUL TRUTH about cats is that they aren't all that much FUN because they sit around sleeping most of the time.

ZZZZZ   ZZZZZ

Dogs are the opposite to cats.
They like lots of movement.

WHOOSH!

WHOOSH!

WHOOSH!

WHOOSH!

WHOOSH!

WHOOSH!

Dogs can be FUN
because they like
to watch TV
with you.

They like to play games with you.

They like to come into the car with you.

Given half the chance, they would like to do everything with you.

The AWFUL TRUTH about dogs is that they want to go on having FUN for ever and ever.

READY FOR MORE

COMPLETELY EXHAUSTED

SWOOSH SWOOSH

HOOT AND HOWL'S AWFUL TRUTH REPORT			
HOOT! ON... MEDIUM-SIZED ANIMALS HOWL!			
TINGLE FACTOR	THRILLING FACTOR	OUCH! FACTOR	AAAARGH! FACTOR
★ ★ ★	★	★	★

The biggest animal you are likely to have FUN with is the horse or pony. The FUN of being on a pony is that you can imagine yourself in the Horse of the Year Show or the Grand National.

However, there are one or two AWFUL TRUTHS you should know about having FUN with horses.

First of all, you have to catch your horse. This is when the horse shows it has a great sense of humour. At least it is having FUN.

Then you have to load up the horse with lots of things – saddles, bridles etc.

Then you have load yourself up with special clothes.

HAT

JODHPURS

BOOTS

Some horses can be very dozy. They might be safe to ride but they won't be much FUN.

FLIES

DUST

AGE : 105

BLIND IN ONE EYE

BAD BREATH

DANDRUFF

LIMP (FRONT) →

← LIMP (BACK)

Other horses are very frisky.

SWIFT ACCELERATION

SMOOTH RUNNING

SHARP BREAKING

SCREEETCH!

This friskiness might lead to a fall. The AWFUL TRUTH is that it will be more of a slow slither. This will be very embarrassing, especially if people are watching.

Lastly, there is the FUN of taking off your jodhpurs. The AWFUL TRUTH is that jodhpurs aren't meant to come off at all.

If there is no one around to help you peel them off you'll have to hook them round something and pull yourself out of them.

HOOT AND HOWL'S AWFUL TRUTH REPORT
ON... LARGE ANIMALS

HOOT!

HOWL!

TINGLE FACTOR	THRILLING FACTOR	OUCH! FACTOR	AAAARGH! FACTOR
★ ★ ★ ★	★ ★ ★ ★	★ ★	★ ★

THE AWFUL TRUTH ABOUT FUN WITH WHEELS

Hoot and Howl have got themselves a pair of wheels, they want to find out the AWFUL TRUTH about FUN and wheels.

Bikes are good FUN. To have FUN on a bike you need a helmet that's the right size.

You need a bike. Like the helmet, this shouldn't be too small . . .

. . . or too big.

You need balance. This is very important. The AWFUL TRUTH is that if you don't have balance you will hit the pavement.

CLUNK!

You will hit other things, too . . .

LAMPPOSTS

TREES

GDUNK!

KERBS

FLOWERBEDS

If your balance is really bad, the AWFUL TRUTH is that you will need an extra pair of wheels which is no FUN at all.

HOOT AND HOWL'S AWFUL TRUTH REPORT

HOOT! ON... BIG WHEELS HOWL!

TINGLE FACTOR	THRILLING FACTOR	OUCH! FACTOR	AAAARGH! FACTOR
★ ★	★ ★	★ ★ ★ ★ ★	★ ★

If you are going to use rollerblades
you will have to look really *cool*.
The AWFUL TRUTH is that you have
to wear lots of protective gear which
makes being cool very difficult.

YOU WILL NEED...

ELBOW
PROTECTORS

WRIST
AND
HAND
PROTECTORS

KNEE
PROTECTORS

HELMET

If you really want to be safe, you need . . .

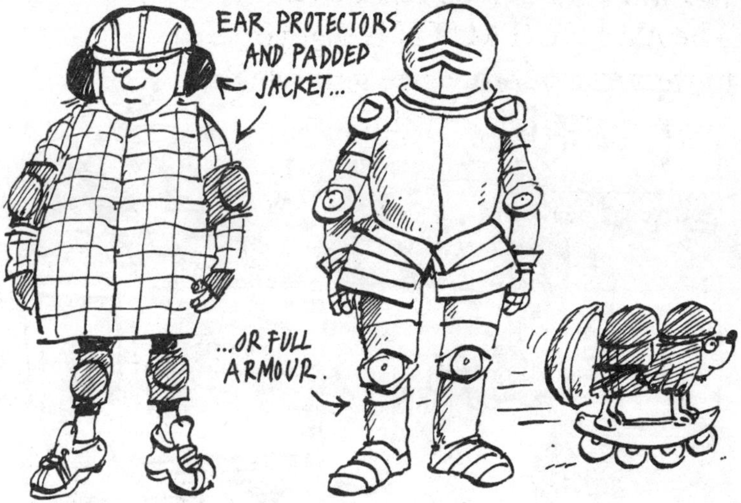

EAR PROTECTORS
AND PADDED
← JACKET...

...OR FULL
ARMOUR.

To stop FUN turning into FUNGE on rollerblades,
remember the golden rule – keep your legs together.

CORRECT

WRONG

You have to be careful not to post yourself or bin yourself.

You have to watch out especially for:

a) Little old ladies with wheelie bags.

b) Dogs on the end of long leads.

c) Dog poo.

SLURPSH

HOOT AND HOWL'S AWFUL TRUTH REPORT			
HOOT! ON... SMALL WHEELS HOWL!			
TINGLE FACTOR	THRILLING FACTOR	OUCH! FACTOR	AAAARGH! FACTOR
★ ★ ★	★ ★ ★ ★ ★ ★	★ ★	★ ★

THE AWFUL TRUTH ABOUT THE FUN OF COLLECTING THINGS

Hoot and Howl have collected a few facts about collecting.

HOOT!

HOWL!

Collecting is very popular and lots of people find it FUN. Some people do it every day. Some people collect stains on their tee-shirts . . .

SIMON'S STAIN COLLECTION

SPAGHETTI SAUCE (2 HELPINGS)

FOOTBALL MARK (FOUL)

DOG PAW MARKS

FOOTBALL MARK (TACKLE)

GREEN PAINT FROM SCHOOL PROJECT ON TREES

TRICIA'S GREEN PAINT AFTER SIMON SAID TRICIA'S TREE WAS RUBBISH

FIZZY CAN OF JUICE

SOMETHING SIMON'S MUM WILL GET VERY ANNOYED ABOUT

FOOTBALL MARK (GOAL SAVE)

Some people collect things on their shoes.

CHEWING-GUM

ODD LACE

BIKE OIL

DOG TOOTH MARKS

SMALL STONES THAT GO 'CLICK, CLICK, CLICK'

SOMETHING DISGUSTING

MUD (GARDEN)

MUD (LANE)

MUD (PLAYGROUND)

STICKY WRAPPER

Some people collect things in their schoolbags. In fact, they have collections of things in their collection

BITS-OF-OLD-LUNCH COLLECTION (IN ORDER OF AGE)

APPLE (THIS WEEK)

BIT OF BISCUIT (LAST WEEK)

CRISP (WEEK BEFORE LAST)

DUSTY PEANUT (LAST MONTH)

SOMETHING COVERED IN MOULD (LAST YEAR)

SWEET WRAPPER COLLECTION

CRUMB AND FLUFF COLLECTION

JOTTER COLLECTION

PENCIL-CASE COLLECTION

PENCIL SHAVINGS COLLECTION

OTHER ITEMS COLLECTION

TERRY

SQUASHED SPIDER

BIT OF ANCIENT STICKING-PLASTER

DOG BISCUIT

CASSETTE

ONE AND A HALF SHOE LACES

TAPE THAT SHOULD BE IN THE CASSETTE

But now for the serious collections. The AWFUL TRUTH is that some people get carried away with the FUN of collecting.

Ben has 480 things with a picture of his favourite footballer, Greg Backnett, on them. Here are a few:

FACE FLANNEL

PEN ↘

CURTAINS →

SOCKS ↘

FLOOR RUG ↘

UNDERPANTS ↘

SOAP ↙

BUBBLE BATH ↙

Tracy likes collecting furry things, like slippers or pencil-cases or teddy-bears. This might be FUN for her but not for anyone else.

REAL DOG WITH HAYFEVER BECAUSE OF TOO MUCH FUR →

Making collections is fun while it lasts but it has to come to an end sometime.

I think I'll stop collecting football mags. and stickers.

HOOT AND HOWL'S AWFUL TRUTH REPORT

HOOT! ON... COLLECTING THINGS HOWL!

TINGLE FACTOR	THRILLING FACTOR	OUCH! FACTOR	AAAARGH! FACTOR
★ ★			

THE AWFUL TRUTH ABOUT FUN AND THEME PARKS

Hoot and Howl are getting very excited. They are going to a Theme Park to see how much FUN and how much AWFUL TRUTH there is.

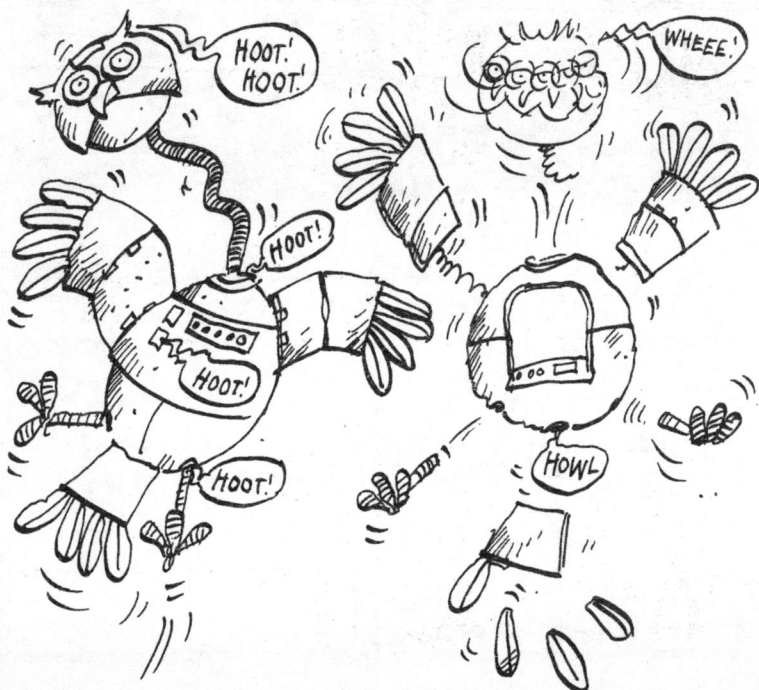

There are three things you do at a Theme Park:
a) Queue
b) Eat
c) Do things that make you wish you hadn't eaten.

You will have to queue to get in. The AWFUL
TRUTH is that this might take a long time as the
queue will stretch round the world two times.

BUS STOP
FOR BUSES
TO END
OF QUEUE

After queuing for such a long time you will
need refreshments.

Then you will go to Jungle World and try the
River Ride where you will be . . .

WHIRLED...

...WHOOSHED...

AND FINALLY
DROPPED
DOWN A
WATERFALL

Then it's time for another refreshment.

After that you will go for a wander in *Dracula's Castle* where you will be . . .

SLITHERED ON BY SLIMY THINGS...

...AND SHRIEKED AT BY BONY THINGS

WHAA... "AAAAA!

And now it's lunch-time.

Then it's a ride of the *Circle of Doom* (three times) where you will be . . .

...TURNED...

...SWIRLED...

...SWOOSHED..

At the end of it you have to check you are all in one piece and that you haven't lost anything. An amazing amount of things disappear on the *Circle of Doom*!

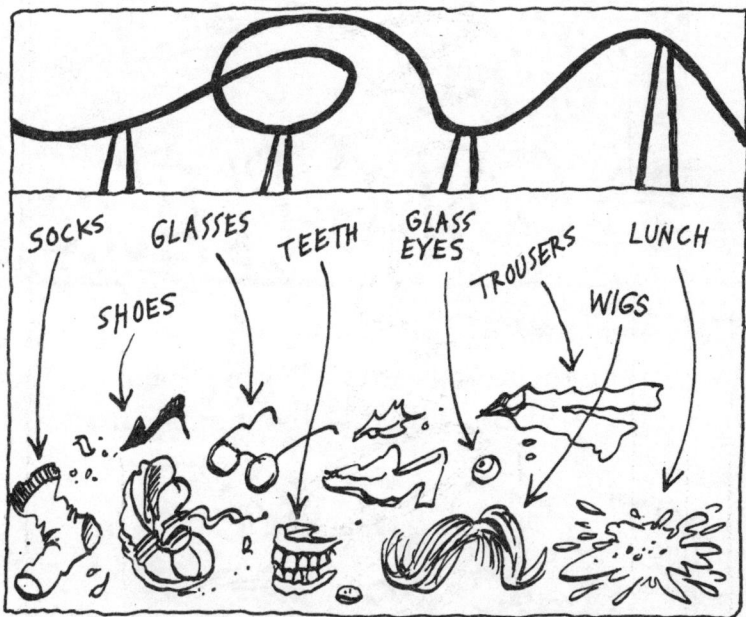

SOCKS GLASSES TEETH GLASS EYES TROUSERS LUNCH

SHOES WIGS

The AWFUL TRUTH about FUN in Theme Parks is that you can have too much of good thing.

HOOT AND HOWL'S AWFUL TRUTH REPORT

HOOT! ON... THEME PARKS HOWL!

TINGLE FACTOR	THRILLING FACTOR	OUCH! FACTOR	AAAARGH! FACTOR
★★★ ★★	★★★★ ★★★ ★		★★★★★★ ★★★★ ★★★★ ★★★★ ★★★

THE AWFUL TRUTH ABOUT FUN GOING PLACES

Hoot and Howl are packing the suitcases and their picnics and their sunglasses. They are going to check up on the AWFUL TRUTH about going away.

There always seems to be FUN in other places.
The windows of your local travel agent will be full
of posters and brochures showing people having
lots of FUN.

When you get ready for going somewhere grown-ups can get quite tetchy. They rush around a lot . . .

. . . and they squawk a lot.

Have you got..?

Squawk!

Do we need..?

Squawk!

What have you done with the..?

Squawk!

Shall we take..?

Squawk!

You haven't forgotten the...?

Squawk!

We're going to be late!

Squawk!

The AWFUL TRUTH is that the FUN hasn't started yet and it maybe some time before it does. The grown-ups will do some more squawking.

The next stage is to get where you are going to. Hoot and Howl have looked at the FUN of different ways of travel.

TRAVEL BY CAR	
EXERCISE ★	
FOOD ★ ★ ★	
FUN ★	

SQUEARK SQUEARK

EXERCISE

NOT MUCH EXERCISE BECAUSE YOU ARE STRAPPED TO YOUR SEAT. YOU CAN EXERCISE YOUR ARMS IF THE WINDOWS ARE STEAMY AND NEED WIPED.

I feel sick

FOOD

PROVIDE YOUR OWN.

FUN NOT MUCH TO DO EXCEPT WATCH THINGS WHIZZING BY — WHEELS, TREES ETC.
IF YOU'VE GOT A BROTHER OR SISTER YOU CAN THROW THINGS AT THEM OR HAVE AN ANNOY-SOMEONE COMPETITION.

BUS OR COACH	
EXERCISE	★
FOOD	★ ★
FUN	★ ★ ★

EXERCISE

NOT MUCH EXERCISE EXCEPT BOUNCING UP AND DOWN ON YOUR SEAT.

FOOD

PROVIDE YOUR OWN. IF YOU'RE ON A SCHOOL TRIP YOU CAN EAT EVERYTHING AT ONCE. (THIS WILL MAKE YOUR RUCKSACK LIGHTER BUT YOU'LL BE HEAVIER.)

FUN

YOU CAN HAVE GREAT FUN WITH YOUR FRIENDS, SING SONGS AND TELL RUDE JOKES. SOMETIMES THE DRIVER WILL TURN UP THE RADIO REALLY LOUD.

YOU CAN LOOK AT THE BACK OF THE DRIVER'S HEAD BUT HE'LL BE WATCHING YOU IN HIS MIRROR — SO BEWARE.

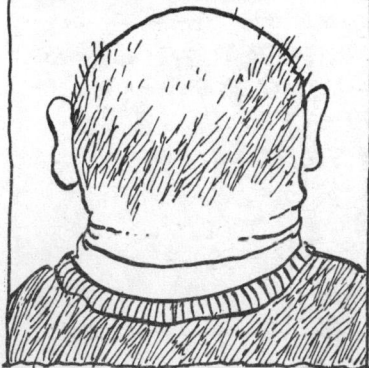

PLANE		
EXERCISE	★★★	
FOOD	★★★	
FUN	★★	

HOOT!

GATES 16-20

THE AWFUL TRUTH ABOUT TRAVELLING BY PLANE IS THAT YOU MIGHT HAVE TO DO A LOT OF WAITING AT THE AIRPORT. THIS ISN'T MUCH FUN.
SOMETIMES THERE ARE LONG DELAYS AND YOU MIGHT HAVE TO WAIT FOR AGES AND AGES.
YOU CAN ALWAYS GO OFF FOR A WANDER ROUND THE AIRPORT (SHOPS, NEWSAGENTS, AMUSEMENTS) BUT REMEMBER...

...DON'T GO TOO FAR AWAY!

EXERCISE

ONCE YOU'RE ON THE PLANE YOU CAN EXERCISE BY WALKING TO THE LOO LOTS. YOU HAVE TO WATCH OUT FOR THE CABIN STAFF WHO LIKE TO MOW PEOPLE DOWN WITH THEIR TROLLIES.

FOOD

PROVIDED BY AIR COMPANY IN PACKETS YOU CAN'T OPEN

FUN

YOU MIGHT GET AN IN-FLIGHT MOVIE. OTHERWISE YOU'LL HAVE TO ADMIRE THE VIEW... (DEPENDS WHERE YOU'RE SITTING.)

a) PERSON ACROSS THE AISLE.

b) BACK OF SEAT.

c) CLOUDS.

TRAIN	
EXERCISE	★★★★
FOOD	★★★★
FUN	★★★★

HOOT! HOOT!
HOWL!

EXERCISE

YOU WILL HAVE TO HELP CARRY THE LUGGAGE WHICH IS GOOD WEIGHT-TRAINING. YOU CAN WALK UP AND DOWN THE LENGTH OF THE TRAIN GOING TO THE LOO OR BUFFET CAR OR COUNTING CARRIAGES.

FOOD

YOU CAN COLLECT THINGS FROM THE BUFFET-CAR IN LITTLE PAPER CARRIER-BAGS.

FUN

YOU CAN PLAY GAMES ON THE TABLE BETWEEN THE SEATS. YOU CAN COUNT THINGS AS THEY PASS THE WINDOW, LIKE SCARECROWS, COWS WITH THREE LEGS, ODD NUMBERS OF SOCKS HANGING ON WASHING-LINES ETC., ETC.

FERRY

EXERCISE ★★★★★

FOOD ★ ★ ★

FUN ★★★★★★

HOOT HOOT!

UPPER
DECK
←

FERRIES ARE GREAT
FUN AND GREAT
EXERCISE. YOU CAN RUN
UP AND DOWN STAIRS AND
ALONG DECKS.
FOOD - CAFETERIA AND
        SHOPS.
WEATHER WARNING -
FERRIES CAN GO UP AND DOWN.

HOOT AND HOWL'S AWFUL TRUTH REPORT

HOOT! ON... GOING PLACES HOWL!

TINGLE FACTOR	THRILLING FACTOR	OUCH! FACTOR	AAAARGH! FACTOR
★	★★		

THE AWFUL TRUTH ABOUT FUN WHEN YOU'VE GOT THERE

What sort of FUN can you have when you reach your destination? Hoot and Howl have been looking around.

The seaside is a favourite place for people to go and have FUN. Here is some of the equipment you'll need to enjoy the seaside . . .

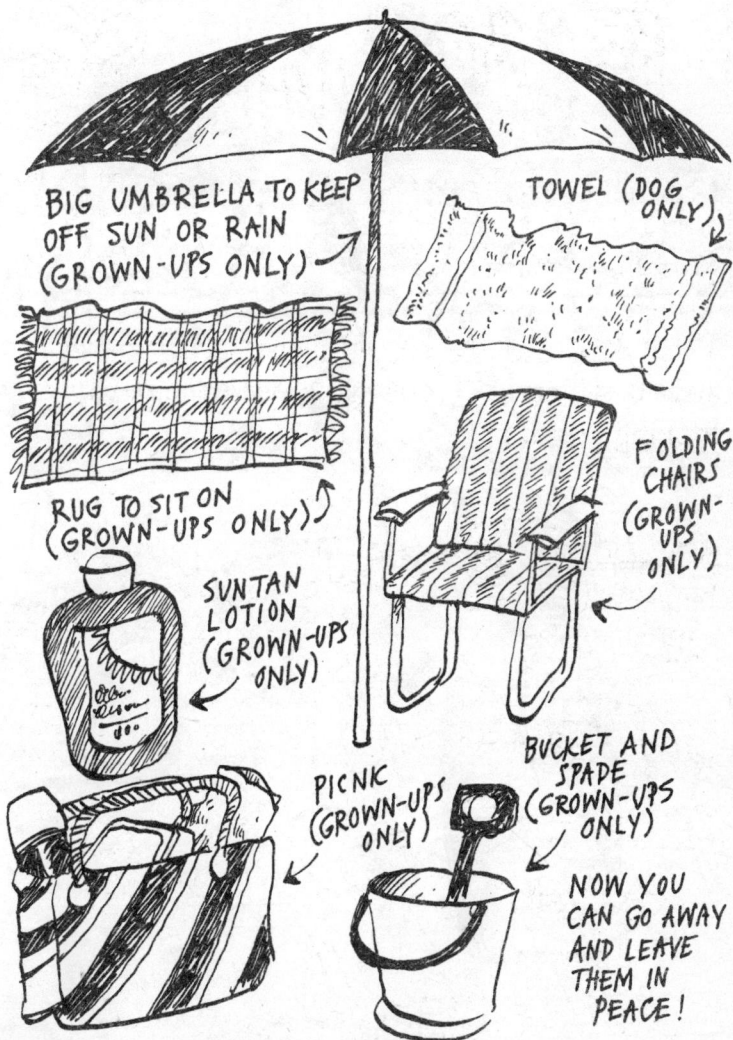

BIG UMBRELLA TO KEEP OFF SUN OR RAIN (GROWN-UPS ONLY)

TOWEL (DOG ONLY)

RUG TO SIT ON (GROWN-UPS ONLY)

FOLDING CHAIRS (GROWN-UPS ONLY)

SUNTAN LOTION (GROWN-UPS ONLY)

PICNK (GROWN-UPS ONLY)

BUCKET AND SPADE (GROWN-UPS ONLY)

NOW YOU CAN GO AWAY AND LEAVE THEM IN PEACE!

But the AWFUL TRUTH is that . . .

. . . lots of other people will have the same idea about going to the seaside.

If you want a bit of space to have FUN you might have to put on your swimming-costume and go into the sea. Sometimes the sea can be very cold.

Then someone will make you even colder . . .

There are lots of creatures down there in the water. Some are fierce and some are slimy.

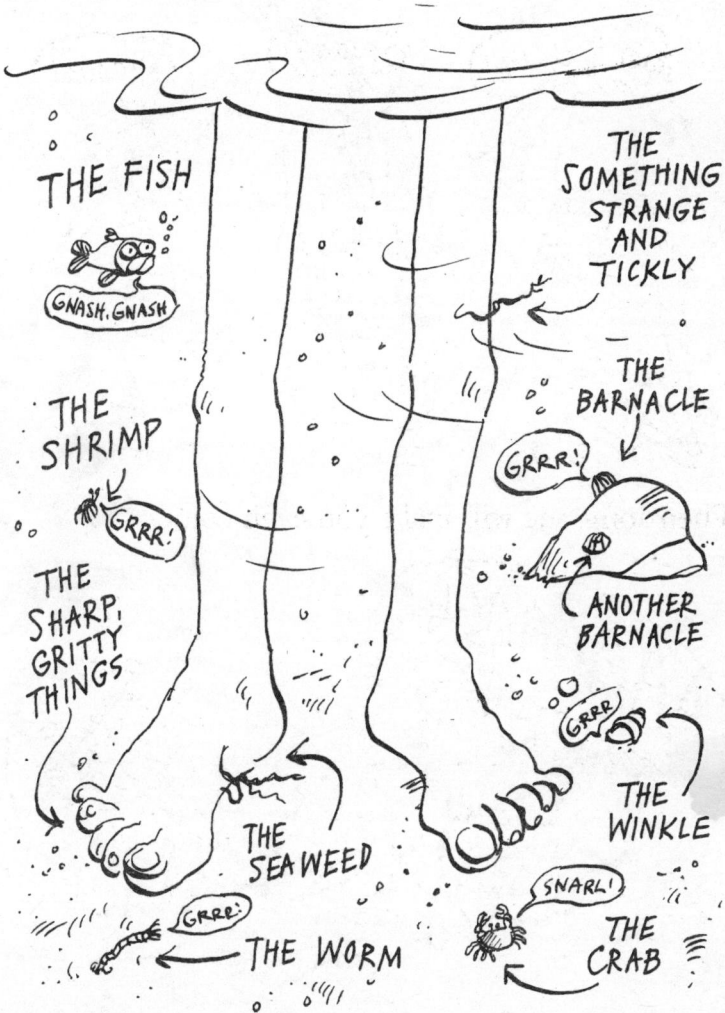

And worst of all . . .

... the **SHARK!**

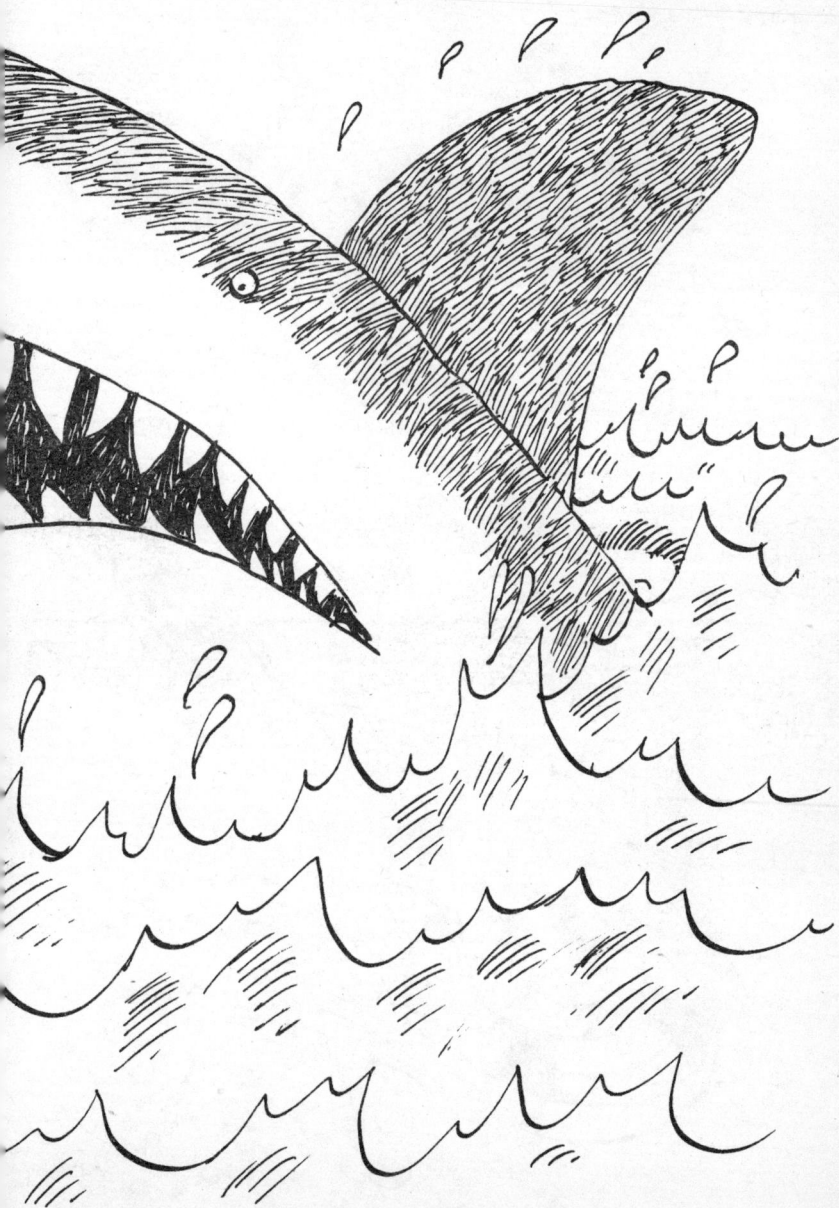

The AWFUL TRUTH is that other people will be
having FUN in the water which might not be FUN
for you.

When you get out of the water you will be like
a sand magnet and sand will stick to you everywhere.

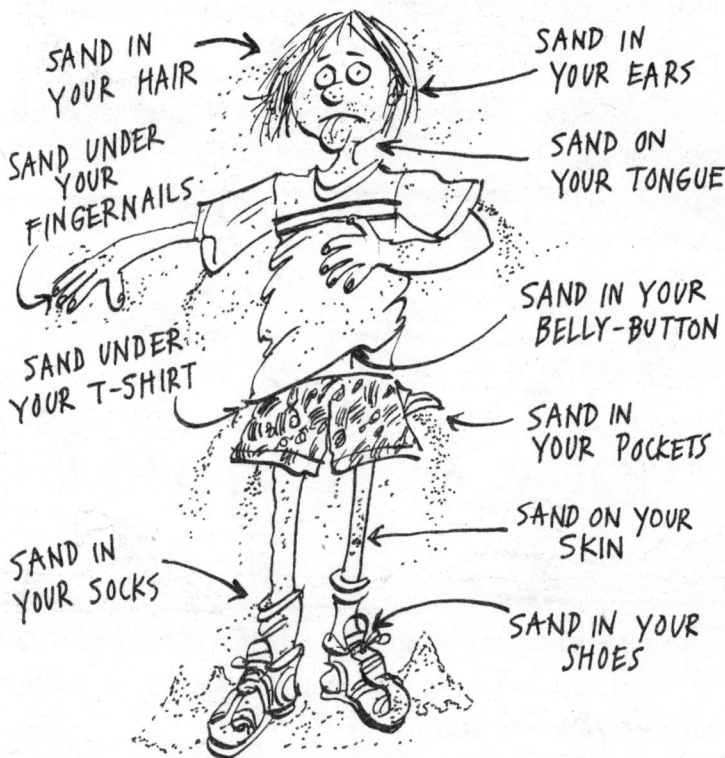

SAND IN
YOUR HAIR

SAND IN
YOUR EARS

SAND UNDER
YOUR
FINGERNAILS

SAND ON
YOUR TONGUE

SAND IN YOUR
BELLY-BUTTON

SAND UNDER
YOUR T-SHIRT

SAND IN
YOUR POCKETS

SAND ON YOUR
SKIN

SAND IN
YOUR SOCKS

SAND IN YOUR
SHOES

Worst of all will be the sand in your SANDWICHES
which will make them strange and crunchy.

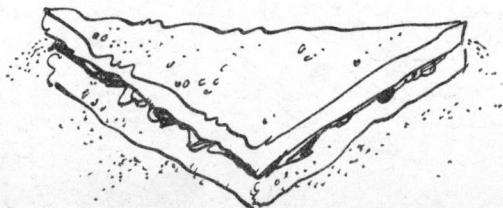

There are lots of other places where you might want to go to have FUN. Hoot and Howl have been taking some photographs of people having FUN.

These people have gone to an ancient castle or historic house. They were hoping to run around and look for ghosts.

These people have gone to an historic house. The AWFUL TRUTH is they had to listen to a guide nattering on for hours.

These people went camping so they could have FUN putting up the tent and having a barbecue.

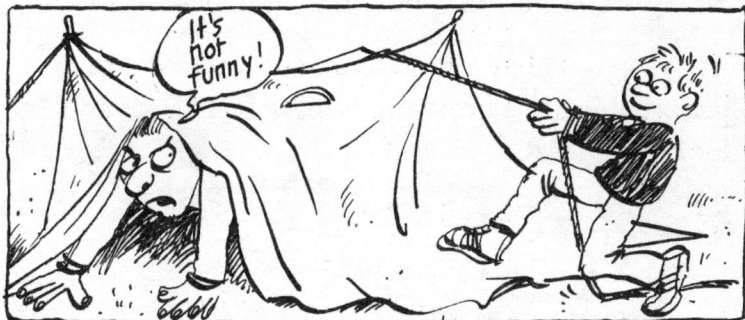

The AWFUL TRUTH is that they had to put up with some other things . . .

BURNT SAUSAGE

LEAKING TENT

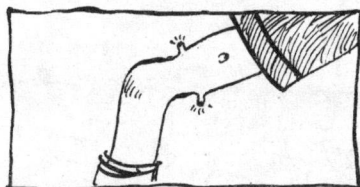

MOSQUITO BITES

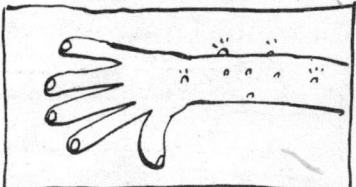

MIDGE BITES

SMELLY ANIMALS

SOMETHING WRIGGLY IN THE BOTTOM OF YOUR SLEEPING-BAG

These people went to enjoy the FUN of sightseeing in another country.

The AWFUL TRUTH is that their FUN turned into FUNGE and worse.

ARGUING ABOUT WHERE TO GO

ARGUING ABOUT GETTING LOST

ARGUING ABOUT WHERE TO EAT

So here is Hoot and Howl's final selection of AWFUL TRUTH photographs:

THE FUN OF GETTING TO THE TOP OF A MOUNTAIN JUST WHEN THE MIST COMES DOWN

THE FUN OF GOING SKIING WHEN IT SUDDENLY BECOMES VERY MILD

THE FUN OF GOING TO THE AQUARIUM WHEN THE SEA-CREATURES ARE HAVING A DAY OFF.

HOOT AND HOWL'S AWFUL TRUTH REPORT

ON... WHEN YOU'VE GOT THERE

TINGLE FACTOR	THRILLING FACTOR	OUCH! FACTOR	AAAARGH! FACTOR
★ ★	★ ★ ★	★	

THE AWFUL TRUTH ABOUT FUN AND GAMES

Hoot and Howl are flexing their muscles. They are going to find out how games can be fun.

HOOT!

HOWL!

Games come in all shapes and sizes. Pushing and pulling is one of the easiest game to play.

It's the sort of thing you do in your school classroom. However, the teacher won't like it and she'll spoil the FUN by shouting at you.

If I have much more of these fun and games, there will be trouble!

Computers are great FUN but the AWFUL TRUTH is that they have some bad habits. Here are a few of them:

The Big Freeze-up: The picture will freeze on the screen. No matter how much clicking you do, the computer isn't listening because its thinking of something else.

Pea-brain: You bring home a new computer game (oh, excitement!) but your computer will have none of it.

Gobbledygook: This shows that computers have a weird sense of humour. Instead of printing what you want, they print nonsense.

Heh, heh, heh!

Never-never-ending: This is when you *always* get stuck at *exactly* the same point in a game *every time*. The computer just does this to annoy you.

Why can I *never* get the Lord Dragonostril into the Kingdom of the Seventh Level?!

Tsk, tsk! Are we getting a little over-heated?

Lots of games are played with balls. The AWFUL TRUTH is that you have to be very careful you don't get on the wrong side of these balls or the FUN will end.

Games are usually played with at least one other person (or a computer if you can't find anyone else.)

They are played on a board . . .

. . . a field or court . . .

. . . or a chunk of countryside.

The AWFUL TRUTH is that often you won't be able to play on the right kind of field with the right kind of people.

GOALIE

GRANDSTAND

SEAN'S BRILLIANT HEADER

PLAYER

FANS

REFEREE

SUBSTITUTE

PLAYER

LINESMAN

You will just have to make do as best you can.
This will be more challenging and more FUN.

ANOTHER OF SEAN'S BRILLIANT HEADERS

PLAYER

PLAYER

PLAYER

PLAYER

PLAYER

PLAYER

SEAN'S BRILLIANT GOAL

GOALIE

The AWFUL TRUTH about games is that the FUN sometimes includes injury. Here's a game you can play: look at the injured people on this page and guess how they got their injuries. The answers are on the opposite page.

(A) MONOPOLY

(B) GOLF

(C) CANOEING

(D) FOOTBALL

(E) COMPUTER GAME

(F) CRICKET

C CANOEING – HE FELL OUT OF THE CANOE AND WAS POKED IN THE EYE BY A DUCK.

E HE GOT VERY EXCITED WHILE PLAYING A GAME AND ACCIDENTALLY KICKED THE CAT WHICH BIT HIM.

YESSS!

F SHE WAS ABOUT TO CATCH A BALL WHEN A BEE GOT IN THE WAY.

A SHE HAD AN ARGUEMENT WITH THE OTHER PLAYER AND HE STUCK THE DICE UP HER NOSE.

It's a double six!

B HIS GOLF BAG WAS TOO HEAVY AND IT FELL ON HIM

SPLAT!

D SHE WAS HIT ON THE HEAD BY THE GOAL-SCORER (WHEN HER BOOT CAME OFF).

GOAL!

HOOT AND HOWL'S AWFUL TRUTH REPORT

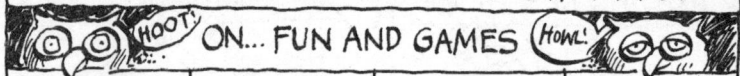

HOOT! ON... FUN AND GAMES HOWL!

TINGLE FACTOR	THRILLING FACTOR	OUCH! FACTOR	AAAARGH! FACTOR
★★★	★★	★★★★	

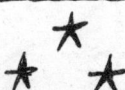

THE AWFUL TRUTH ABOUT FUN AT HOME

Hoot and Howl have been peering in windows and doors to see what sort of FUN can be had at home.

You can have quite a lot of FUN at home. First of all you exercise yourself.

You can trampoline on a bed.

Double beds are even better.

If you've got a brother or sister or a friend to stay you can go raiding.

You sneak out of
your room and across
to theirs.

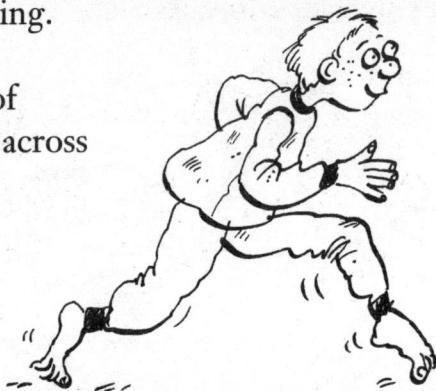

You rush in and rush off with their bed clothes.

SWURSH

Of course, they will come to get their own back so you'll have to be ready for them.

You can have FUN with grown-up stuff. You can paint your face with make-up . . .

or try shaving foam sculpture.

You can turn the sitting-room into an *Adventure World* assault course.

CABLE CARS

HEADQUARTERS

STOREROOM

JUNGLE AND WILDLIFE

DEADLY SNAKES

You can have a marathon obstacle race with your pals.

See how long it takes to get all the washing off the line (with one hand).

See how long it takes to run downstairs, open the fridge and take out a yogurt (with no hands).

See how many times you can carry a bag of
pop-corn round the kitchen (on your head, on
one foot).

See how high you can throw a tomato and catch it
again (with your eyes shut).

To finish with you can have FUN in the bath. You can add lots of nice smelling things from the bottles in the bathroom.

Then you can turn on the radio and just lie back and relax.

The AWFUL TRUTH about FUN at home is that grown-ups don't think it's FUN at all . . .

. . . and they may spoil it for you by going all funny.

HOOT AND HOWL'S AWFUL TRUTH REPORT			
HOOT! ON... FUN AT HOME HOWL!			
TINGLE FACTOR	THRILLING FACTOR	OUCH! FACTOR	AAAARGH! FACTOR
★	★ ★	★ ★	★ ★

THE FINAL AWFUL TRUTH ABOUT FUN

Hoot and Howl have tired themselves out with too much FUN. Their computers have gone a bit crazy with all that hard work but here is their last report . . .

If you've lost the ball for your fun-ball set don't think it would be FUN to use the cat instead. It's fur will clog up the gloves.

If you think it would be FUN to give the dog a trim and a perm remember the dog might get a shock when it learns the AWFUL TRUTH.

If you think it would be FUN to send your granny into outer space, make sure she's got her pension book, her specs and a packed lunch.

The AWFUL TRUTH is that she might come back with an alien body-guard.

There is no limit to the FUN you can have with . . .

A SANTA CLAUS BEARD

A PIRATE'S EYE PATCH

A PAIR OF JOKE FALSE TEETH

SNACKA-SNACK

A COUPLE OF FOOTBALLS

A PAIR OF TIGHTS STUFFED WITH PAPER

A SLICE OF ORANGE PEEL

The AWFUL TRUTH about FUN is that you will still be having it when you're 105.